The
Referral
King

The Referral King

MIKE STERANKA

5 Star Marketing
MILLERSVILLE, MD

For information contact:
www.mikesteranka.com
8530 Veterans Highway, 2nd Floor
Millersville, MD 21108
443.308.5216

ISBN: 978-1-939758-00-2 (trade paperback)
ISBN: 978-0-9836406-4-6 (ebook)

Printed in United States of America.

CONTENTS

Acknowledgments

Many people have to be thanked for their input with this book, but none more so than my mother Dorthy Steranka. My mother encouraged me, supported me and in many ways allowed me to experiment with life while keeping a loving and watchful eye on me. Thanks Mom for all of your words of encouragement.

Professionally and personally I would like to thank Jane Sinclair, the President of Retirement Planning Services, Inc., for her dedication and support over the last several years. I could not have done this without you.

To my friends Sterling Spell, Ralph Moores, and Daryl Colbert—thanks so much for twenty plus years of laughs and tears…and for showing me true friendship.

And to the countless financial advisors I have had the privilege to coach over the last several years. Keep those text messages coming as it brightens my day knowing I was able to show you how to be more productive.

Foreword

When I explained my referral concept to a senior executive of the third largest insurance company in the world, he encouraged me to get it printed and published, and to teach it to every industry. He said the process was so good that it could be transferred to several industries simultaneously. It is for that very reason that the book seems generic with its approach to the referral process.

When you visit **www.mikesteranka.com,** you will be able to purchase a very specific approach used for professionals in the financial services arena. It is my desire that you visit the website, make the purchase, and start to receive the hundreds of fantastic referrals I receive each year.

I hope that you incorporate the paradigm shift that I speak of in every marketing, sales, and service campaign that you employ in whatever industry you find yourself in. You will start seeing results in just a short time, and they will truly blow you away.

After many years, you will recognize that you truly have no competition because your learned "concierge level of service" has made your business the Ritz-Carlton of that industry.

As you transition into this new way of thinking, your business will become clearly defined quite naturally as you find your niche a little bit more each year. You might find that you spent a lot of time and money in the past in areas that were not congruent with your business model, your staff, or your client base. Using the new approach that I suggest, will most certainly identify those problem areas so they can be corrected.

Lastly, *The Referral King* was written for you—the consummate sales professional—looking to improve your service, your sales and your "referability" factor. Enjoy.

CHAPTER ONE

Referrals, a Definition

What makes a successful business or career? Networking? Hard work? Simple luck? There are plenty of theories on what will bring in clients and profits, but if you want to see real growth in your company or your employer's company, the one practice you cannot afford to ignore is the power of referrals.

Why?

Because if you're a business owner or a sales representative, your most profitable return on investment for your own business or your employer's business is a referral. That may seem like a strong statement, but referrals are the best—and possibly only—way to make your business or career a long-term success. The cost is virtually nothing; a referral is essentially goodwill that you've created by carrying yourself in a professional manner.

...I've developed goodwill because I've done what I said I would do or the products and services that I've offered have done what I said they would do.

Let's say I've handled all of my client transactions, whether they be brand new or many years old, in a professional manner. As a result, I've developed goodwill because I've done what I said I would do or the products and services that I've offered have done what I said they would do. When I ask for a referral from that client, there should be very little resistance, and because the acquisition cost is nothing more than the goodwill I've built up by being a professional, it will save me countless hours of chasing bad leads and my employer thousands of dollars in marketing to find new clients or a prospect for me to speak to. It's that easy, but nevertheless few people seem to know about the power of referrals.

TAKING THE TIME

Though referrals are the most efficient way for a business to grow, they are often the most overlooked as well, because people are too busy handling the actual client relationship to take the time to consider asking for a referral. What I am proposing in this book is a paradigm shift—introducing the referral aspect into the client relationship in your sales presentations, your prospecting methods, and your ongoing servicing of that client. By introducing the referral component into the relationship, in fact just by mentioning it, you will be carving out time for it.

Say I am meeting with a prospect, and I spend my entire time—an hour or two hours—just trying to wow them and forgetting to take a moment to ask for referrals. Ultimately I'm shortchanging myself. I'm also potentially shortchanging my client, because he has friends or business associates who could benefit greatly from the services I provide. If I never bring up the subject, we lose the momentum that could be created by introducing the referral into the sales presentation and servicing aspect for that client.

In this book I'll discuss the importance of making referrals a priority in your life and in your clients' minds. That doesn't necessarily mean the client is going to be able to refer you at all times, but if you plant some awareness in the consumer's mind that the way

I'm also potentially shortchanging my client, because he has friends or business associates who could benefit greatly from the services I provide.

...you're not only carving out time for referrals, you are actively taking steps to keep your business out of a rut and bringing the referral back to the position of prominence where it belongs.

you want to operate is by dealing with other nice and professional people just like him or herself, then they're going to recognize that, and when they're in a conversation with one of their friends or business associates—nice and professional people just like themselves—they'll think of referring you. Therefore you've done your job and created that mind awareness in your client's head. Whether they refer you immediately or not, they will think of you.

As I mentioned earlier, we are a busy lot; whether we are business owners or sales reps. In this day and age we are bombarded with everything from cell phones to the Internet to text messaging to fifteen second advertisements on television. We are in a twenty-four-seven-totally-connected-have-to-be-on-at-all-times society. What that does is beat us down, so much so that we want to turn off. We suddenly decompress because it's too much activity, too much noise, too many text messages, and too many phone calls.

Because of this onslaught, we get into routines. Those routines can turn into ruts, and ruts can be very deep. If they get too deep we can get stuck; we get stuck in a rut and we don't even know it. However, by introducing the referral aspect into your marketing, prospecting, sales presentation, closing, product or servicing delivery, and ongoing client relationships, you're not only carving out time for referrals, you are actively taking steps to keep your business out of a rut and bringing the referral back to the position of prominence where it belongs.

THE COST OF DOING BUSINESS

In today's business world, the cost of acquiring a new prospect or client has increased tremendously. Yet how much does a *referral* cost?

Nothing.

Let's say that five years ago a business owner spent two hundred dollars in order to secure a new client. Now that cost has risen to eight hundred dollars—that's a four hundred percent increase. However, if the business owner talked to that new client and got a referral, suddenly that acquisition cost drops from eight hundred to four hundred. Why? Because that client offers another name, and that new name in turn becomes a new client.

Is that businessman now competitive in the marketplace? Absolutely. His competitors are still paying the eight hundred dollars for a new client while he's been able to cut his operating costs in half through referrals. If he gets a referral from an

Your highest and best usage of your marketing dollars in nearly any industry in the world is going to be on your client base.

existing client and there was no acquisition cost other than a first phone call, a postcard, or maybe a dinner meeting, he has a very low acquisition cost. What's the rate of return on something he's paid nothing for? It's exponential.

Your highest and best usage of your marketing dollars in nearly any industry in the world is going to be on your client base. So think of this: Let's say I'm a professional. I have my own small business, and I have a hundred clients. Now let's say my marketing budget is fifty thousand dollars for the year. I could spend that fifty thousand on advertisements to try and bring in new people, a strategy resulting in ten to fifteen new clients a year.

However, instead of spending that entire fifty thousand on trying to draw in new clients, I could also take a portion of that money, maybe thirty thousand dollars, and spend it on my existing clients in a number of different ways. I could have special events such as guest speakers or dinners. There are so many different things you can do once you know who your clients are and where their interests lie.

So if I spent that thirty thousand on my clients, and 80 percent of those hundred attend one of my feel-good events, they would be happy. As a result, if they were properly approached they would give me referrals—more than enough referrals to easily equal my entire annual revenue generated from going after cold prospects.

With that said, if I spend my remaining twenty thousand dollars just going after cold prospects and I only pick up ten new clients, while from the thirty thousand I spent on my existing clients I pick up twenty new clients, I've spent the same fifty thousand but am ahead by fifteen clients. Moreover, my clients are happier because I have gone over and above in my service by providing events they enjoy.

WORLD CLASS SERVICE
LEADS TO WORLD CLASS REFERRALS

Over the years I've posed the following example to my staff. I put a set of china with nice silverware, a nice wine glass, and a nice drinking glass in front of them. Next to that I set a paper plate with a plastic fork and a shoddy napkin. I then ask which they would prefer to use. Most people choose the china. Why? Because it's nicer.

First-class service works the same way. If you're offering higher end goods, you must offer higher end service. You must. It's an absolute. Whether that service relates directly to your business is almost inconsequential. What's important is that the client knows that you're there and you're trying to continue to bring value to the relationship. When they see that value being brought to the relationship, they're very, very happy. When they are very, very happy, they are apt to refer you.

It doesn't just happen overnight, though. You can't simply say, "Okay, I'm going to ask for referrals from everybody I meet." You have to build up that goodwill I talked about earlier and make sure it's in place before asking for the referral. How do you do that? You take a survey. You know the pulse of your clients and you continually meet with them to make sure that you have happy individuals. When you have happy individuals as clients and customers, you can approach them and ask for referrals or personal introductions. If you are taking the necessary steps, you will be like a laser beam cutting through steel. You will be extremely competitive, more profitable, and happier.

A FAILURE TO LAUNCH

Most business owners spend far too much time seeking new clients, which is expensive, instead of seeking referrals from existing clients which is, as I've said, essentially cost free. So why do people stay stuck in that mindset when they know that referrals are a better way to go?

There are actually two reasons. One is that they just don't think about it. As I mentioned above, most people are operating in a twenty-four-seven world. They're running from one commitment to the next: "I've got to go get the kids, drop the kids off, work a twelve-hour day, answer emails, respond to text messages. Oh, and I read that book on referrals, but ugh, I'll get to it tomorrow." But tomorrow turns into two years from now practically overnight.

We all know how time flies. In the blink of an eye we're two years older and our kids are now graduating and we're saying, "How did that happen?" Or the kids are driving, or the kids are saying, "I want you to pay for college." Or the kids are graduating from college and saying, "Hey, I want to go to medical school." Suddenly you look in the mirror and you have grey hair. We don't think about time passing, and before long it's too late—the business has gone under or the career has ended because we didn't take the simple step of asking for referrals.

The second reason is fear; people are simply afraid to ask. It all goes back to building up that goodwill. If a business owner or sales rep suspects that the goodwill isn't there, they

We don't think about time passing, and before long it's too late—the business has gone under or the career has ended because we didn't take the simple step of asking for referrals.

...if I don't do what I say I'm going to do or if the products and services I've sold don't deliver the way I purported they would, I'm less likely to be confident enough to ask for a referral.

may be reluctant to ask for the referral or personal introduction.

For example, if I always have someone answering the phone at my company versus a voice mail maze that confuses people, I'm giving world-class service. If I'm giving world-class service, I don't have any trepidation about approaching a client and asking for a personal introduction.

On the flip side, if I don't give world-class service, if I don't do what I say I'm going to do, or if the products and services I've sold don't deliver the way I purported they would, I'm less likely to be confident enough to ask for a referral. In sales and marketing it's all about confidence, and the representative has to have confidence in what they are doing or what they are selling to their clients. If I'm big on sales but terrible on service, I can't come back and ask for more introductions because, although I sold the best gadget in the world, I wasn't there to pick up the phone and service the account. I never sent a follow-up. I never sent a survey. I never sent anything, and now there is no store of goodwill.

Consider this situation: if I sell a fence to a client and, five years later, find that business is slowing, I may call that client and say, "Hey, it's Mike. I know you bought a fence from me five years ago. Do you need a new a gate for that?" The client might respond, "You know, it's funny you should ask because I just bought a gate a year ago from a guy that I'd never done business with, but he called me every year just to see if I was ready for a gate. He knew that eventually I would need one, so he stayed in touch with me." Again, the goodwill was never built up, so the referral never materializes. It's fear of this kind of rejection that leads many people to avoid asking for referrals in the first place.

GOING THE DISTANCE

In the following chapters, I'll outline all of the steps you will need in order to ensure the success of your business or career through the use of referrals. However, the most important thing to remember before embarking on this process is that you absolutely must embrace a new way of thinking.

What I've done in this book, and in the coaching I do in a number of industries, is map out a thought pattern that you must follow. If you follow this thought pattern and introduce it as I suggest, you will get very positive results. If you try and skip some steps and do only, say, two out of the ten steps I give you, your program is likely to fail.

By introducing these steps in sequential order to your business practices, you will have a new way of life—more referrals, higher profits, lower acquisition costs for clients or prospects, and more profits in your bank account. That is the power of referrals.

For more information, please visit

www.mikesteranka.com

CHAPTER TWO

Getting Referrals

Now that you know exactly what a referral is and how important it can be to the survival of your business or career, it's time to take a closer look at exactly how to get them. In the first chapter I talked about introducing referrals into the mindset of the sales representative or the business owner, but now it's time to commit 100 percent to getting those referrals. In order to do that, you're going to follow a pattern of action that I will outline here, starting with what steps you need to take to get referrals and personal introductions on a regular basis.

Step one in the referral process is simply this: making the commitment as a business or an individual to go through this entire process. Write it down. Make a contract for yourself. By doing that, you are putting down on paper that you are committed to following through. There is something powerful

...the main reason people don't get referrals is simply because they don't ask. They don't ask because they don't know how to ask.

that comes when we put pen to paper and start thinking, and I know that as a business owner, when I put something down in writing, I generally make sure it happens. This is the promise you are making to yourself and your business—to use the referral process as a way to increase your clients and therefore your profits.

THE ART OF ASKING

As I've already mentioned, the main reason people don't get referrals is simply because they don't ask. They don't ask because they don't know how to ask. They don't know how to ask because no one ever taught them how to ask. No one taught them how to ask because no one really thought about it, or no one put any effort into it. They didn't put any effort into it because they didn't know how to approach it. They didn't know how to approach it because they didn't know what's involved. They didn't know what's involved because they didn't know the processes.

What I'm going to do now is walk you through that process in order to show you how it will fit into your new way of thinking. Again, as I said in the previous chapter, if you stick to only two of these steps, you will not be successful. You will have some short-term achievement, but it will not be long lived. I'm going to teach you something that, once you apply it, you'll be able to take into any industry. You'll even be able to take it to your community and use it for things such as fundraising for non-profits or other community activities. This will enter both your business and personal lives. It's going to be fantastic.

As I said before, we are going to introduce this way of thinking into five different areas—marketing, pre-approach, sales presentations, closing, and any ongoing servicing and/or delivery. As we do this, something is going to happen. You're going to start seeing referrals from an entirely different view. The whole point of this process, and one of the reasons I've been so successful in getting referrals and turning them into clients, is that I have confidence in my well-thought-out approach. If you have a referral plan that is well thought out, even the naysayers, the people who have said to you in the past, "I never refer anybody," will come over to your side of the equation.

On one occasion some time ago, I was meeting with a new client. When I asked him for a referral, he responded, "No, I'm not going to do that. I'm not going to just give you some names." I said, "Okay, did I say something incorrect? Or have I not serviced your account properly?" He said, "Oh, no, nothing could be further from the truth. You've provided excellent service and I love what we've done with your company. My point was simply this: I'm going to get a group of fifteen of my friends together, and I want you to come out and present to them the same way you presented to me—one on one." I said, "Okay, I can do that."

The reason I share that story with you is because it illustrates how one little conversation can lead you in a direction that can make you hundreds of thousands or even millions of dollars in referral fees or commissions. It's easy. Again, all we have to do is ask. Now let's look at those five areas of ongoing daily business where referrals can easily be introduced.

MARKETING

The first area is marketing. When we introduce the referral aspect into marketing, any pieces that we distribute as a company should reference the fact that we accept referral business. In fact, if we actually have the data that shows that 56 percent of our business last year came from referrals, I would put that in my advertisements with a line that might read something like this: "Joe's Plumbing: 75 percent of our business last year came from direct clients."

If we don't know the exact percentage of revenue that came from satisfied customers through referrals, we could simply say something like: "Joe's Plumbing: We do business the old fashioned way—by word of mouth. We appreciate all the referrals that we've received over the years." We could even follow up that line with a quote or testimonial from one of those satisfied customers.

That's just one example of how to introduce the referral aspect into a company's marketing campaign. There are several other methods which I touch on in the samples located at my website (insert web address), but no matter which tactic you use, it is very important to introduce the fact that you accept referrals, anticipate referrals, and need referrals for the livelihood of your business.

...any pieces that we distribute as a company should reference the fact that we accept referral business.

PRE-APPROACH

The second area where you should introduce the referral aspect is on your pre-approach. The pre-approach takes place prior to having a meeting with a prospective new client or customer. It could be anything from flyers that are handed out to a salesperson's elevator pitch. It could be as simple as running into a potential client and saying something like, "Our business is doing fantastic; we get

The big problem for a lot of people with referrals is that they don't have a system, or they occasionally do something that works but then stop.

so many referrals because people are satisfied with the type of work that we do. So if you're ever in need of the service or product our company provides, please give us a call."

Adding just a few simple lines can be as easy as that, but the effect can be exponentially powerful. In both the marketing and the pre-approach, if you always mention referrals it will become ingrained in your prospect or client's mind. Soon, they too will expect to be asked for referrals, so your approach won't be a surprise.

The big problem for a lot of people with referrals is that they don't have a system, or they occasionally do something that works but then stop. The beauty of adding a referral aspect to each of these areas is that you are introducing it in all aspects of your ongoing daily business, creating a culture for it in your company, and alerting all of your clients and potential clients that this is a major part of how you generate revenue. In fact, it may even help you create business when a potential client falls through.

Let's say your business involves giving prospective customers a quote. After meeting with a potential new customer and offering them a quote on the service you could provide for them, you could say something along the lines of, "Most of our business comes from referrals, so we hope you like this quote, and by the way, if you know of anybody else who could use our services, please feel free to let us know."

In both the marketing and the pre-approach, if you always mention referrals it will become ingrained in your prospect or client's mind.

That is a very powerful statement. There will be some people who will say, "Well, you haven't even earned the business yet, so why are you asking for a referral?" But let's say somebody never intended to use your quote; they just needed to get three different quotes in order to compare. However, it turns out they like you because you are honest and have a good business. So when you ask if there is anyone else they can speak to, they might say, "Well, my neighbor really needs some help. In fact, they've called two or three companies already but haven't found anyone they liked." And with that, you have a new potential client.

It's such a simple thing to add to your process, yet it can yield so much. Nevertheless, as I mentioned in the previous chapter, it is paramount that everyone in your company be enmeshed in this type of approach.

SALES PRESENTATION

The next area where we will introduce referrals is the sales presentation, when we actually present our product or service to a potential new customer. As with the other areas where the referral aspect has been introduced, adding it to the sales presentation is as easy as including a few simple sentences that could go something like this: "Sally, we think you'll absolutely love the type of service that we do. In fact, most of our customers are people just like you who have referred us to other people they know who could benefit from this, and we would hope that down the road, if you become a satisfied client, you too will refer us to people who you know."

If you approach the situation like this, don't be surprised when your prospect says, "It's interesting you should say that, because we've been talking to our neighbors about the types of products and services you offer, and they are also in the market for XYZ but haven't been able to find anyone to fill the bill. They've asked us to keep them posted on our dealings with you, and I think they would end up coming to see you if we end up doing business with you."

The reason that is happening is because consumers are more discriminating than ever before. These days many people take their time in making decisions, even talking to other people in this decision-making pro-cess—which makes introducing the idea of a referral all the more important.

It takes about five seconds to say that line, but the results can be fantastic. That extra effort is what separates the superstars from other people; the superstar spends that extra five seconds, but he does it with a purpose.

"...If you're pleased with your experience with our company so far, is there anyone you can think of at this time who might benefit from our services?"

CLOSING

The fourth area of introduction is the closing. At this point you've marketed your business, pre-approached a potential client, and given them a sales presentation or two. Now they have decided to move forward and it's time for the closing.

Those final moments, as you're finishing the last of the paperwork, might go some-thing like this, "Sally, I'd like to thank you for your business. We really appreciate this and look forward to servicing you on an ongoing basis. If you're pleased with your experience with our company so far, is there anyone you can think of at this time who might benefit from our services?"

Then simply be quiet and listen to what they have to say. Chances are, if you've been planting that seed along the way, six times out of ten times you're going to have them say, "You know what? You should call my friend Steve. He has a similar need and I told him about you. He's anticipating your call." Again, you can see how introducing the referral aspect into every level of your daily business can have a profound effect.

ONGOING SERVICE AND DELIVERY

The fifth and final part of this process could potentially be the most powerful of all, and that's ongoing service and delivery. Ongoing service and delivery is simply this: If I sell a product or service and someone has a question, concern, or problem, we need to address that.

Let's say you sell fences. You've just finished installing one on a client's property, and the client, having inspected it, is pleased with the result. That's when you would go in with the following line: "Bob, it's been so pleasurable to do business with you. Your fence looks fantastic. You'll be the envy of the neighborhood. I'm sure you know other people you've been talking to about your fence. Is there anyone you think could benefit from getting a new fence or talking to us at this time?"

Again, just be quiet and see what Bob says. He'll say yes or no. If he says yes, that's good. If no, okay, you can come back to that at a later time. Either way, you haven't lost anything by asking and you may have actually gained a potential new customer.

Where this could be potentially the most powerful is if you're in an industry that offers customer service in any way, shape, or form. If you properly train your service personnel with specific lines, you can generate millions and millions of dollars in referral business.

Imagine, for example, that you own a company that manufactures and sells windows. One day a customer calls unhappy or dissatisfied with one of the windows because there's a defect with the product. Your customer service person takes the call and schedules a time for the issue to be fixed. They then do a follow-up call to the customer once the problem has been resolved, and the call goes like this: "George, I understand we've fixed your window today. Well, I'm so glad we could do that and, truly, at XYZ Windows we care about your business and are glad we could be

> If I sell a product or service and someone has a question, concern, or problem, we need to address that.

of service to you today. Is there anything else we can help you with as relates to your windows?"

If the answer is no, the customer service representative goes on: "George, we really appreciate your business. Would there be anyone else you know of who could benefit from XYZ Windows?" Again, be quiet and listen. The person is either going to say yes or no. If they say yes, they have a name. If not, you haven't lost anything but a few seconds of your time.

So to recap, what we've talked about is introducing the referral aspect in your marketing, in your pre-approach activity, in your sales presentation, in your closing, and in your ongoing service and delivery. If you introduce it in that fashion, you will be very successful in your referral endeavors.

GET IN THE MINDSET

The question I get asked most often is, "Does this really work? Will people actually refer me business?" My answer to that is yes, it will work; but you must change your mindset and your attitude towards referrals.

Think of it like this: You must have a passion for what you do as a sales representative. You must believe explicitly in the product or service that you deliver. If you do not believe one hundred percent, I would suggest that you quit your current position and pursue something that you do believe in. However, if you truly believe in the product or service you deliver, and you're so passionate about it that you own one yourself and your friends and family all own it as well, you actually feel, as a sales representative, that you're doing your client a disservice by not providing it to everyone they might refer.

That is where the paradigm shift comes in.

In the financial world, I'm very passionate about what I do. I'm very good at it and I want to protect as many people as I can. I want to show them the ways in which I have successfully done that. Therefore people that want what I am offering, which is safety, are apt to refer me to other friends who want the same kind of safety. That will absolutely happen with your business as well, but it's very important that you change your focus if it's not one hundred percent positive towards the referral approach.

We are human beings, and our world can change rapidly. If you hang around negative people you will get negative results. If you hang around positive people you will get positive results. So who are you choosing to hang around?

> You must believe explicitly in the product or service that you deliver. If you do not believe one hundred percent, I would suggest that you quit your current position and pursue something that you do believe in.

> If you hang out with people who are making more money, I can tell you that you will make more money.

A wise mentor once told me that our income five years from now will largely be determined by two things: the books that we read over the next five years and the people we associate with over that same amount of time. So I would ask you those questions as well. First, what books do you plan on reading? Books such as this one can help improve your professional revenue tremendously.

Next, who do you plan to associate with over the next five years? If you hang out with people who are making more money, I can tell you that you will make more money. I can also tell you that if you hang out with people who make no money, in five years you will make no money. That's pretty much a fact. It's all about your mindset, and if you believe in this referral process, your business will immediately begin to show the gains.

LOOKING AHEAD

As we move forward, I encourage you to start thinking about the chart found at my website, which illustrates those five areas where referrals will be introduced, because eventually you are going to add a line or two to every advertisement that you do, every conversation that you have, every presentation that you make, every closing that you do, and any delivery and/or servicing that you undertake. At the website you can also find information on additional consulting you can enjoy, which I'll come back to at a later time.

Initially this will all feel like you're throwing a baseball with your left hand if you are right-handed. Eventually, however, it will become second nature, and as it becomes second nature, you'll realize there is no other way to conduct your affairs than to add referrals as an integral part of your business life.

For more information, please visit

www.mikesteranka.com

CHAPTER THREE

Monetizing Your Referrals

At this point in the process, you have introduced the referral aspect into all levels of your daily business, from your marketing to your customer service. You have gone the extra mile to satisfy your clients; they love the product or service that you provide, and many of them have given you a list of referrals.

So now what? How do you turn those referrals into clients and revenue?

GETTING TO KNOW YOU

In many ways, depending on what product or service you sell, the process of turning a referral into a client is just as much an art as actually getting the referral in the first place. However, if I am selling a product or service where the commissions are several thousand to tens of thousands of dollars, that's a little

Ultimately, the art of handling the referral is simply determining as much information as you can about that individual from the person who referred you.

bit different than handling a referral where the commission is a hundred dollars or less. For the purposes of this book, I'm specifically talking about referrals that can garner a few thousand or tens of thousands of dollars in commissions or fees.

Ultimately, the art of handling the referral is simply determining as much information as you can about that individual from the person who referred you. How old is he? How does your client know him? What type of money does he have? You have to ask whatever questions are necessary and appropriate to the product or service you are offering. In the financial world, for example, I get very detailed because I want to know as much about the referral's financial situation as possible.

Start off by asking your client for the best way to get in touch with the referral. How well does he or she know the referral? If your client's spouse was throwing a surprise birthday party, would the referral be invited, or is he more a casual acquaintance? These are questions you can ask to find out how close the association is.

For example, I was with someone recently and asked how well he knew a referral he had given me. "Well," he said, "we used to work together." As I questioned the man further, I learned that, though he had retired and the referral was still working, the two men still met for coffee each week. Okay, now I know that he meets this person on a regular basis. "What do you guys talk about?" I asked. "Life, marriage, career, retirement," the man told me. So now I know that my client is referring me to a trusted confidante that he meets with each week for coffee for thirty to forty minutes, and they talk about life, marriage, career, retirement, dreams, goals, aspirations, fears, health, sickness, death, you name it, the list goes on and on. That is what I would consider a very good referral.

When you get the name of a person, you want to find out as much information as possible. If the people are unwilling or unable to furnish you that information, that is not a true referral. It is simply a name. In that case, you might mention to your client that you are looking for a referral with whom they have a stronger relationship, someone they feel may truly have a need for the services or product you offer.

FROM REFERRAL TO CLIENT

Now that you know as much as possible about your new referral, turning that referral into a client is a whole other thought process. In fact, just because they are a referral doesn't mean

> I've found that once I've identified that the referral has a need, we close them 85 percent of the time.

they will become a client. For instance, they may have no need or desire for the product or services that you deliver, but maybe somebody was so impressed by you that they referred you to everybody they knew even if they didn't have a need for your services. The main thing you have to do is have a conversation with that referral to gauge their level of demand.

I've found that once I've identified that the referral has a need, we close them 85 percent of the time. That's because I've asked those questions, I've determined a need, and I was able to fill that need. That happens on a routine basis at my company, and it can happen at your company, too.

But how do you go from referral to client to revenue?

One of the most important things you can do right off the bat is to write down and fix in your mind and in the minds of your staff what a qualified referral looks like for your business. What do they sound like? What do they smell like? What kind of car do they drive? How do they lean politically, if that's important? Once you have that picture in your mind, you can share that with your clients, and more than likely that picture is reflected back in them since they've already done business with you.

Now I will say this, sometimes people will refer you to somebody who looks like them and thinks like them but isn't like them at that time. What that means is that the referral is a qualified person with potential, but they are not highly qualified at that exact date. They could be highly qualified six months from now or six years from now or somewhere in between. So you have to make a decision as a company as to how you will handle that qualified referral.

At my firm, we would put them into a system and do a follow-up, staying in touch with that person until that six-month or six-year deadline came to pass and they became highly qualified. With that said, there might be an opportunity for you to do business with them immediately, though on a much smaller scale.

For example, let's say you sell a product or service that is a big ticket item, but they

One of the most important things you can do right off the bat is to write down and fix in your mind and in the minds of your staff what a qualified referral looks like for your business.

just aren't in the market for that at the moment. However, they are in the market for something else, and your company offers that something else. That something else might be one or two percent of the ultimate purchase price of the big ticket item, but its true worth is in showing your client that you have the ability to service the needs that go around that bigger ticket item, and you've demonstrated the level of care to actually mention this.

Generally when you're introduced to a qualified person who isn't qualified yet, there may be a product or service that you can offer to them immediately. You still might make a few dollars—not as much as when they become highly qualified—but you could get your foot in the door. That's the most important thing. Once your foot is in the door you can, with permission, go back and market to them, you can send them newsletters, you can invite them to events, and they are likely to have friends similar to the friends who referred them. It's all part of the same client-referral cycle.

BREAKING THE CYCLE

By now you have clients, and those clients have given you referrals which you have identified as the type of qualified potential clients you would like to pursue. The referrals may or may not have need of your services immediately, but you have stayed in touch with them and possibly even helped them with smaller issues that have allowed you to get a foot in the door and maybe even some more referrals. As I mentioned above, it's all part of the same cycle. You have a client and provide good service. Because you give good service, that client gives you a referral. Because the referral is qualified, they become a client. The new client gets good service and they give a referral. The referral becomes a client, and so on.

What can break that chain is if you don't take care of their referrals. Because I've been in business for a long time, I've had instances where this has happened, where my company has not taken the proper care of a specific referral. It might happen once in a thousand times, but when it does you feel terrible.

Several years ago, I happened to run into a client outside of the office. When I asked him about a referral he had once given me, the client responded that he had indeed passed the name along, but that I had never called the referral. I was floored and immediately apologized. "Wow," I said, "I can't believe we didn't call them. I apologize. Is it okay to reach out

You must also be respectful of the people to whom you are referred.

to them again?" At first the client was a little skittish, but eventually they agreed that I could re-approach.

At the time that the referral fell through the cracks, my company was going through a personnel change, and I believe that's when the slip occurred, but that's no excuse. It's my company. The responsibility lies directly with me. In that case I re-approached the referral and they became a client. Above all, it's very important that you take care of the people who refer you.

You must also be respectful of the people to whom you are referred. As an example, let's say a client refers you to someone who is a difficult personality, and you recognize that there is no chance you're going to do business with them because of that difficult personality. However, that doesn't mean you shouldn't be pleasant and respectful towards them. In this instance a simple, "We really appreciate the chance to meet you," will suffice.

You don't have to follow up with phone calls or emails or invites to different events or newsletters, but you do need to avoid offending them, because the thing that will stop those referrals from happening is not being respectful of the people to whom your clients refer you. If they send you one of their good friends and you are difficult, it reflects poorly on them.

REFERRED BY THE REFERRED

So is it possible to ask a referral for a referral?

Absolutely.

In fact, they're probably waiting for you to ask. Why? Because that's how they got there in the first place. Some of my best clients were third or fourth generation referrals; meaning Bob became a client, he referred Joe, Joe referred Nick, and Nick referred Pete. Now Pete is an advocate who endorses me to everyone he meets. You never know when that's going to happen. It's just like looking at different fruit trees. Why do some branches produce more than others? I don't know. Maybe the light hits them better. Maybe there was a little more care given or water supplied. Nevertheless, some branches will naturally bear a bit more fruit than others.

At the website you'll find a referral tree I've put together to help you keep track of these connections. The chart will be a huge help in mapping out the Bob to Joe to Nick to Pete type referrals. Once you've put that chart together, you must always be cognizant of it, because what if you're three generations deep into it and you have a falling out with Nick. Well,

Nick was referred by Joe who was referred by Bob. So Nick might go back to Bob and Joe and say, "Hey, my experience was no longer good."

A situation like that can kill a whole branch of referrals if you don't pay attention to it. However, if you water it and nurture it and give it the proper time and attention, then it will bear the fruit it has already shown it can.

For more information, please visit

www.mikesteranka.com

CHAPTER FOUR

Ask and You Shall Receive

Studies have shown time and again in industry after industry that satisfied consumers will recommend a purchase nearly 80 percent of the time if they are simply asked. However, people don't ask, and if they don't ask they don't receive.

We've already talked about the various reasons why a person may not ask for a referral. Nevertheless, the consumer really wants to share his or her experience, and if you just look around the world today, with the advent of Facebook, Twitter, LinkedIn, and all the social network media that's available, you're seeing people commenting on their experience.

What we hear about most often are the unpleasant experiences because they get the most publicity. It's said time and again that a dissatisfied customer will tell five people while a satisfied one may tell only one or two. That's why it's so important to get a handle on your clients and your customers, find out their level of comfort with what you have positioned in their lives, and ask them for a referral. In four out of five cases, if you ask, they will say yes.

PERSONAL INTRODUCTIONS

There are actually several ways to ask for that referral, and one of the best is the personal introduction. Let's say you're in the closing phase with a new client. Now that you've introduced the referral aspect at all levels of your business routine, you've been planting the seed in your client's mind ever since the marketing phase. You have successfully delivered your product or service, your client is pleased, and you take those extra few seconds to ask, "Joe, do you know anyone else who you think could benefit from the services I provide?"

Because Joe is so pleased with the service he has received, he is more than happy to give you several referrals. However, you can now take the referral process one step further and ask for a personal introduction. It's much cleaner. It's much easier. It's smoother and it can roll off your tongue.

Instead of simply asking for that list of names, in this case you might say something along the lines of, "Joe, if we were in a business setting and a few of your coworkers walked by, would you introduce me?" When Joe responds that he would, you can go on to ask how he might do that. "Well, I would tell them that you are my financial planner." To which you would respond, "Okay, that's simply what I want you to do, Joe—give me some personal introductions to some people you know."

At the website we have several different sample scripts for personal introductions. They work, they're time-tested, and they've brought me millions and millions of dollars in product sales. I would suggest that you too use those personal introductions because they will make you a lot of money.

> At the website we have several different sample scripts for personal introductions.

REFERRAL LETTERS

Referral letters are another great way to take the referral aspect one step further. In my own business, referral letters have always been an integral part of our process, and when I systematized my business and co-authored the book The E-Myth Financial Advisor: Why Most Financial Advisory Firms Don't Work and What to Do About It with E-Myth guru Michael Gerber, that referral letter process was systematized along with everything else.

Again, you can find samples of referral letters at the website, but here is how the

"Recently I've done some business with Sally, and she recommended that I send this invitation to you."

process should work. Let's say you get five referrals from a client, a list of five names that they think could benefit from the service that you provide, and you decide to send them referral letters.

One of those letters might go something like this: "Dear Bob," it would start, "Recently I've done some business with Sally, and she recommended that I send this invitation to you." From that point on there are several different layers that can be used in the letter. It can be a request for a meeting, a dinner date, a presentation, or even an invitation to a client appreciation event.

In the case of the sample above, you're introducing yourself via a letter. You're saying: "I would just like to introduce myself and here's a little brochure about my company. I have no idea if you're in need of the services that we provide, but we just want to make ourselves available. By the way, we'll be sending you something soon to invite you to a dinner seminar, and if by chance you can join us at one of those seminar dates, be sure to mention that you were referred by Sally, and we'll make a special gesture when you get to the event to say thank you for coming."

By doing it this way, you've logically progressed to a point where it's difficult for the referral to say no if they truly have any need for the types of products or services that you offer. For example, my financial planning firm focuses on retirees; that's who we market to and that's who we get as referrals, and with ten thousand people a day retiring in the United States, it's on everybody's lips.

As a result, a referral letter I send to a potential client may go something like this: "I would just like to say that, whether you're satisfied or not with your current financial planner, come to an event and see if you like what we have to say. If you decide to come in for a personal appointment or consultation, we'll tell you if your retirement plan is perfect or not. If it's perfect, we'll give you our blessing and send you on your way. If it's not, maybe you have a need for a product or service that we offer and we'd like to explore that at a future date. Does that sound fair enough?" Almost without fail people respond in the affirmative.

LETTERS OF INTRODUCTION

Using referral letters or referral invitations to events is extremely profitable and successful. Some of my best clients have come from these referral letters. Nonetheless, another option is

... prepare the letters for them, addressed to their referral, and simply have the people sign them so that you can send them out and take care of the postage.

something called a letter of introduction. The letter of introduction is simply a letter from my client to the prospect. Again, a sample is included at the website, but it works a little bit differently from a referral letter in that it's on letterhead from my client.

Now, while you might have some very pleased clients who are more than happy with the level of service you have provided, you will have very few with the time to actually put together letters on their letterhead and send them out. So what you can do is prepare the letters for them, addressed to their referral, and simply have the people sign them so that you can send them out and take care of the postage.

Keep in mind, however, that this is actually a multi-step process. Once you have the list of referrals from your client, you must get permission from your client to send out the letters. Next, you have to prepare the letters. Finally, you have to have your clients sign the letters before you can actually send them.

Although requiring a bit more work than simply asking for a referral, this process works very, very, very well; it is time-tested and it is proven. So again, if you offer a product or service where you can make five thousand to fifty thousand dollars per transaction, it may be worth the time to do this. I've done it time and again with fantastic results.

All of these referral methods do work, but it's a system that takes time and commitment. Let's say you have a client, and you ask that client for the names of fifty people he thinks might have a need for your product or services. Now maybe that client can only come up with twenty-five names, but that's still a great start. It's really as simple as that.

Yet people don't do these things because maybe they're not comfortable, maybe they don't believe in the product or service they deliver, maybe they don't want to do the leg-work, but what separates Tiger Woods from other golfers or Michael Jordan from other basketball players, or anyone in business who has ultimate success versus someone who has ultimate failure, is that they put in their practice time. They do the extra work that other people don't want to do, and if you prepare

> All of these referral methods do work, but it's a system that takes time and commitment.

these letters and do that extra work, your business will take off.

Going back to those twenty-five names, let's say three of them end up doing business with you. That's three more clients than you had before, and at what cost to you? Nothing more than the time and energy put into asking for the names and the cost of sending out those twenty-five letters. If your average ticket is $30,000, you've just brought in $90,000 for probably less than a thousand dollars in time, effort, and expenses. That's a fantastic rate of return.

KNOW YOUR VALUE

Unfortunately, it seems that most salespeople and business owners stop the referral aspect just as it starts to work. They have some initial success with it and then… nothing. Why is it that so many people stop an obviously winning strategy before they reach true success with it? The answer is simple.

They don't believe they're worth it.

And when someone else comes along and takes that great idea or tactic, making it a success, it's a huge regret. So I would tell everyone reading this book that you are worth it. You deserve it. No one deserves it more than you.

In fact, just by reading this book, you are separating yourself from 95 percent of the world. Most people when they graduate college, or high school for that matter, go on to read only two to four books total in their lifetime. I read between six to eight books a month. By reading six to eight books a month, I become acclimated or turned onto or inspired by all these different ideas. When you realize that whatever you believe you can achieve, you write it down and make a commitment to it. Once you've written it down, it's yours.

If I have a mortgage, am I going to pay my mortgage? Absolutely. I make sure my mortgage gets paid. So why don't I make the same commitment with other areas of my life? Why don't I be the guy receiving the number one award versus the guy sitting in the back saying nasty things about the guy receiving the award?

Nearly everywhere I go on business trips, I'm one of the top producers in my field and I am always asked to speak or share my opinion. Now I'm sure there are people that go to these events who are perhaps jealous of me because they haven't done the things that I've done to consistently be a top producer, but it's because I've sent those letters out, made the extra call, and delivered something when no one expected it that my business is such a success.

> When you realize that whatever you believe you can achieve, you write it down and make a commitment to it. Once you've written it down, it's yours.

What they should be saying, however, is, "How can I provide more service, service, service, service?"

I did those little things that other people didn't want to do, and when you do those other things that people don't want to do and you do them on a consistent basis, you will be extremely successful. So don't let anything deter you. Just go for it. Don't stop improving.

SERVICE BEFORE MONEY

Looking back on my years in business, there was actually a time in my life when I did very little. I was young and I didn't think these kinds of practices were necessary. Because I didn't put in the extra effort, I didn't achieve the success that I wanted, and when I saw other people doing them and achieving the success, I became envious.

It wasn't until a few factors helped to shift my paradigm that I saw how wrong I had been. I started reading a lot of books, personal development books and how-to books, and I started listening to motivational tapes and videos. Before long I began to believe in what I was reading, seeing, and hearing. Soon I found some common themes; by continuing to improve and offering incredible service, I would find money flowing in.

Most salespeople have things backwards—they're worried about money. "I need money to pay my rent. I need money to pay my car. I need money to send my kids to school." Money, money, money. What they should be saying, however, is, "How can I provide more service, service, service, service? How can I give more service so my kids can go to a better school? More service so I can drive a nicer car? More service so I can live in a better neighborhood?"

As Earl Nightingale said in the Strangest Secret in the World, "You can drive down the street of any neighborhood in America and determine from the home the type of service that those people are providing." So if I drive to an area where there are multimillion dollar homes, the people inside those homes are probably providing a boatload of service. Again, it's as simple as that. Service is the answer.

So as it relates to the referral aspect we're discussing in The Referral King, how can you provide better service to your existing clientele if by providing better service you will get more referrals? In my company, every time that we've added a new service we generally take a survey, a sample of which can be found at the website, where we ask our clients a few important questions. What do you like that we do? What do you not like? What do you suggest that we add on as a service? Do you know of anybody who could use our services? Even there you get a little chance to ask for a referral, but more importantly you get the pulse of your clients.

TRAINING FOR REFERRALS

"This is all well and good," you might be thinking, "but how do I get my staff to incorporate the referral aspect into everything they do?" Well, you can start by explaining to them how you create revenue; money comes into your company because people value products and services that you sell. Because they value the products and service that you sell, a commission or fee is generated. That commission or fee that is generated is enough to pay a salary, a rent, and the other incidentals that you need in running the business.

So what you impart to your staff is that the client is vitally important and must be cared for. You must be responsive to the client. You must not be argumentative or difficult with any client. You must understand, appreciate, and respect your clients.

After you've done that adequately, you can focus on the service aspects that are expected of your different staff members. This goes back to the idea of systematizing your business and having procedures manuals, samples of which can be found at the website, for every single position in your company. If you don't have one, I would encourage you to write one, be it for the receptionist, the customer service rep, the sales rep, or the account manager. Everybody should have a procedures manual that they follow.

By now you've talked to your staff, you've educated them on the importance of the client bringing in revenue, and you've stressed the importance of the service they provide that client on behalf of your business. The next step is to tell them about adding referral lines to every aspect of their interaction with the client.

As discussed in previous chapters, that line asking for a referral takes only a few seconds to incorporate into any conversation, but the results are astounding. If you make it a matter of course that every single person in your firm, every single time they talk to a client and every single time they address the concern of that client, asks if there is anyone the client knows who could benefit from the services you provide, you will get a deluge of referrals. And that's fantastic.

To drive the point home further, you can reward your staff people ten, twenty, or a hundred dollars per referral. In fact, there are lots of different ways to do incentives. One

> One year I bought seven large flat screen televisions and I handed them out to members of my staff who had brought in referrals.

year I bought seven large flat screen televisions and I handed them out to members of my staff who had brought in referrals. Because it was a gift, a sign of appreciation for the job they had done over the previous twelve months, it went over fantastically. So there are many ways you can motivate your staff. The only thing limiting you is your creativity.

THE REFERRAL BASED CULTURE

Ultimately, what we're talking about here is building a referral based culture inside your business. The lifeblood of any business is its customers or clients. Without customers or clients there will be no business, but without a steady stream of new customers or clients, there will also be no business. Because marketing is changing as we speak, what's effective today may not be effective five years from now, and what worked five years ago may not work today. It's getting more costly for many businesses to compete. So it's essential that they adopt this culture inside their business. If it's properly adopted, your company will be a business that not only survives but thrives.

Think of Apple. Apple has probably the best customer referral program in the world, with people standing in line for hours and hours to get new products all because of word of mouth. Wouldn't you like that same type of word of mouth about your business—people standing in line for hours and hours just to buy what you sell? It is possible. Maybe they won't stand in line for hours, but perhaps they will wait two or three weeks to get an appointment with you because that's how busy you are. It's very nice to always have a calendar full of appointments in front of you, and you too can experience that.

However, it doesn't happen by itself. You must be committed, just as I discussed early on about buying into it. You have to say, "Okay, I'm going to approach it in these five areas of the new client development cycle," and as you introduce it into your culture, your sales pipeline, your staff training, and your ongoing service, it will become your way of business.

Not only will this culture attract new clients, it will encourage existing clients to voice their concerns if something goes askew, which is very important. As an example, I was passing an existing client in the hall and happened to stop him to ask how things were going. After a brief hesitation, he was comfortable enough to tell me about a change he had noticed at our offices that gave him some concerns.

What it turned out to be was that somebody wasn't doing their job properly. They were new to the firm, and the person who had been training them had been forced to leave early, leaving the new employee improperly trained. The client was used to how the office normally runs, and when it didn't run that way, he knew immediately that something was wrong and pointed it out to me. Because he felt comfortable doing that, I was able to address the problem right away. Had there not been a culture of service and referrals, the client would have gone home stewing about it and possibly never have come back.

At my company we encourage feedback. We want a very transparent relationship. Let us know how we can be of more service. It's really about introducing the culture, buying into it completely, and then taking the time to become proficient at it just like anyone becomes proficient at anything in the world. Before long you will be the superstar of your industry.

For more information, please visit

www.mikesteranka.com

CHAPTER FIVE

Showing Your Appreciation

In the previous chapter, I went into more detail about how to develop a referral based culture with your clients and employees. Now it's time to take a closer look at some tactics that can help you get referrals by showing your appreciation for your existing clients.

REFERRAL EVENTS

There are actually two different types of referral events: the type to which you want to invite referrals and the type specifically designed only for your current clients but at which you want to receive the names of referrals.

For example, you might plan to have ten events over the course of a year: a night at the opera, a wine tasting, a play at a local playhouse, a yacht event, and several others.

1. Invitation Referral Events

The first type of referral event, the kind to which the referral is actually invited, starts by putting together a list of those clients you want to replicate—the ones we discussed in an earlier chapter who are nice, professional people you would like to work with again. Once you have that list, you make an action plan for the referral event program that you're planning for your clients.

For example, you might plan to have ten events over the course of a year: a night at the opera, a wine tasting, a play at a local playhouse, a yacht event, and several others. Next, you invite your clients, saying that you would like them to come to the event, and while it's not necessary that they bring a referral with them, it would be nice if they did.

The important thing to remember is that you don't have to put pressure on your clients to bring a referral to the event. Perhaps the client may not have somebody who can make the event, or maybe they can make a future event. Either way, your client will still come and hopefully spend some time saying good things about you to the referrals brought by other clients.

Ultimately, the purpose of the event is to have good attendance and to create a warm and fuzzy atmosphere. Generally you shouldn't talk about business in any way, shape, or form. In fact, I might suggest something like this at the event—script out a five or ten minute talk about your story; the story being you and why you started your business or venture and what keeps you going. Talk about the fact that you love people and that's why you've gathered everyone together.

Above all, you want to make it clear that you're not there to talk business. You're just there to enjoy the yachting, the opera, the wine, or whatever else the function might be, and you want your clients and their referrals to enjoy themselves as well. You could go on to say that this is a great opportunity to mingle with other clients, and to those who were brought to the event by an existing client, you would just like to shake their hand and say thank you for coming out and joining in the fun. That is a referral event meant specifically

> Above all, you want to make it clear that you're not there to talk business.

> If you want to lay out a referral event campaign, what you need to do is take some time to plan.

for referrals to attend, and it works extremely well. It's like anything else; the more you put into it, the more you will get out of it.

If you want to lay out a referral event campaign, what you need to do is take some time to plan. For example, at my company we make our plans in September or October for the following year. So in September and October I'll get together two to four times with my staff and we'll come up with our program for the following calendar year. Then we outline it, we put it in writing, and we make sure we adhere to it. That's important to note because the one thing you have with your clients is credibility. So if you schedule ten events but then cancel six of them, you lose a little credibility.

Last year my company only cancelled one event out of the twelve we had scheduled, and it was actually due to a weather-related issue. The event was scheduled to be held outside, but we were going through a heat wave at the time. We took a pulse of our clients and found that eight were still interested in coming, but as the heat wave continued, pretty much everyone wanted to stay inside.

We ended up calling those people who had expressed an interest in still coming and told them, "If you want us to do it we will, but it is 103 degrees out and we're worried about safety." Most people completely understood the situation, and we ended up cancelling altogether. However, that was an extreme case. In general, it's very important to develop a plan, stick to that plan, and be happy with any results that come out of it.

In fact, that's the only pitfall to referral events—sometimes the expectation of bringing in a ton of business gets too high. You may bring in some new clients, you may not. No matter what, the event should be a thought process—brand building, so to speak, for clients to become aware of who you are as a person. They get to see you in social settings outside of business, not talking about business, so your personality can shine through.

It's important to keep in mind that these events should be kept congruent with who you are as a person. For example, I'm not a drinker, so when we have a wine tasting

> No matter what, the event should be a thought process—brand building, so to speak, for clients to become aware of who you are as a person.

event, I make sure that other people from my staff who do know something about wine will be in attendance at those events. I'm not going to purport to be a wine connoisseur when I don't know anything about wine, but I have someone in my office who is very knowledgeable on the subject so I send that person. On the other hand, I like luxury cars, so if the event is something to do with luxury automobiles, I could go and tell the clients and referrals about my experiences. In the end, it's whatever your comfort level is.

This particular type of referral event is also a good opportunity to build up some of your access to other clients. At one recent event, we had a client who was big into the opera, so we built him up to the other clients who were attending the event. We said, "If you'd like to get more information, see this gentleman here. He's one of our clients, and he's also a founding member of the opera club." Things like that build the client's esteem, making it more likely that they will put your name out there to people they know. As you can see, this kind of event has two or three times the leverage because you're bringing other people into the mix.

Again, I wouldn't put expectations on how many new clients you're going to get. I would just stick to your plan and over the course of the year, I think you'll easily find, at an absolute minimum, a three to five time return on your investment. That means if you spent $2,000 on ten events, you would bring in between $60,000 to $100,000 minimum on referrals from those events. That's an amazing return.

2. Client Referral Events

The second type of referral event is open only to clients, but the key is to make it such a great event that those clients want their friends to be there—but their friends can only get there if they become a client. I've actually held events where people insisted that their friends come in and become a client just so they can attend that function. Coming up with an experience like that is a very powerful thing.

As I said, this type of event is specifically for clients, but when you send out invitations, you include referral cards. Providing around eight cards, you ask the clients to fill in eight names and drop them into the drawing bowl when they come to the function. If you do it correctly, you can pick up between one and two hundred referrals during a single event.

In general, this could be a bigger setting than the invited referral event. Oftentimes

...the key is to make it such a great event that those clients want their friends to be there—but their friends can only get there if they become a client.

As you do these events on a regular basis, you become more accustomed to what people like about them. Clients have lots of fun and they get to mingle with other clients.

at my company we'll even combine it with our annual client appreciation event—a sit-down brunch on a weekend with two to three hundred clients in attendance. We have a live band, a fantastic mac daddy buffet with roast beef carving stations, omelet stations, and anything else you can imagine for breakfast or lunch. We'll even do an open bar. We always have a photographer to take pictures that clients can then download from our website at a later date. They're professionally done, and the client can send it to Kodak to get a framed 8 x 10.

So it's a pretty neat event, and when we do something like that, it will always bring in referrals. As you do these events on a regular basis, you become more accustomed to what people like about them. Clients have lots of fun and they get to mingle with other clients.

Moreover, it's very impressive when you have a setting like that with two or three hundred people. In fact, most people can't gauge how many individuals are present, so it may look like even more are in attendance. Clients will say, "Wow, we have five or six hundred people here." It's a fantastic sight, making the newer clients feel great because they know they've chosen a strong company and older clients feel great because they see the growth of the business. And again, it's good karma; you're sending three hundred people out into the world and they tell five or six friends about the great time they just had at their brunch with their professional.

Fantastic.

So those are the two types of referral events—one where you're actually trying to physically bring a referral in, and the other that is specifically for clients but with an eye towards getting names of referrals. A lot can be said for the referral events we've done over the years. They've worked quite well and we generally bring in enough revenue that we see a ten to fifteen times return on our investment for hosting an event like that.

GIFTS AND INVITATIONS

Gifts and invitations are another great way to show your appreciation to your clients and bring in some referrals. If you use them in a referral campaign, and again I'm speaking in terms of a high-end sale that would bring in between $5,000 and $40,000 in commissions or fees, the more you can offer to clients as an incentive to refer you to other people, the more likely you are to get people to talk.

And for offering that referral and sending in that name in a postage paid envelope, the client's name will be included in a drawing for a free Apple iPad.

My office has a program we instituted where we send out a monthly newsletter to approximately a thousand households. In that newsletter we include a one page letter that essentially says, "Who else do you know who could benefit from the services that we offer?" And for offering that referral and sending in that name in a postage paid envelope, the client's name will be included in a drawing for a free Apple iPad.

As a result of this program, we generally receive between twenty and thirty names per month. We then do a monthly drawing, and one lucky person receives an iPad. They come into the office to pick it up, we take their picture, and the picture can go in the newsletter the following month. When people see their friends winning an iPad, they want to start sending in referrals as well. It's the gift that keeps on giving. Our return on investment in that program averages about twenty times, so we would consider it very successful.

Keep in mind that the prize doesn't have to be something as expensive as an iPad. Whether it's a higher ticket item or a lower ticket item, the thought process will still work quite well. You can also tailor it around an annual event and have multiple prizes consisting of whatever your imagination and budget can create. Several years back, the grand prize at one of our annual events was a trip to the Caribbean for two on a luxury cruise line. It was fantastic. Everybody wanted to be part of the drawing, which meant we had a flood of referrals.

If you're concerned about the cost, look at the strategy from a business owner's perspective. Would you rather spend money on a marketing campaign that may not work, or would you prefer those funds go to gifts to your existing clients—people that already like you and would be more apt to refer you to somebody else?

As for invitations, I have developed some samples which can be found at the website, but essentially how they work is this: I get a referral from a client, we put that person into our ongoing marketing campaign, and then we send invitations on a regular basis to come to one of our future events. A large percentage

> Would you rather spend money on a marketing campaign that may not work, or would you prefer those funds go to gifts to your existing clients— people that already like you and would be more apt to refer you to somebody else?

of those people who receive invitations attend a future event and become a client.

Just remember, all of this takes planning. So, as I mentioned earlier in the chapter, it's imperative that you sit down every September or October and begin putting some actual thought into the gift and invitation strategy for the following year.

PAYING THE PIPER

By now you're probably thinking that all of this sounds great, but how in the world can you pay for iPads and luxury cruises if you have a smaller or medium-sized business?

Well, how you pay for it is dependent on how much money you make from a transaction. Again, I'm talking about a higher ticket item, but these strategies could be accomplished on a smaller scale; you just don't go quite as fancy. At the other end of the spectrum, if you are selling a larger ticket item or service, maybe you can offer even more elaborate events and gifts.

Look at it this way, it's like the difference between buying tickets for a minor league, major league, or all-star baseball game—the price will be according to the demand in the marketplace. So what you have to do is figure out what your average profit is per client and how much you normally spend as part of your top line revenue in marketing. Then what you do is make a calculated decision to adjust some of those marketing dollars that would normally go to direct mail or lead acquisitions and spend them on a referral approach to your client base. In the end, it's all incremental. You're working from ongoing revenue, not creating new revenue.

As an example, let's say I'm spending $20,000 a month on marketing. In September I sit down with my staff and say, "Let's direct fifteen percent of that marketing budget towards a client appreciation event." So if my marketing budget is $20,000 a month, I can direct $3,000 a month, totaling $36,000 a year, towards a campaign. Then I can ask, "Okay, what would our clients like us to do, and what do they like to do, and how much do those events cost?"

Following such a strategy, you might end up only having four or five events, but you might be surprised what you can pull off for as little as five hundred dollars. In fact, for five hundred dollars you could put together an ice cream social and invite one hundred and fifty people. You can rent out an ice cream parlor for two hours and fill it with your clients.

In the end, it all depends on your budget. You could spend a hundred dollars a month,

In the end, it's all incremental. You're working from ongoing revenue, not creating new revenue.

Many of the traditional marketing methods, such as press media, don't work as well as they used to.

ten thousand dollars a month, or anywhere in between based on your availability of funds. Get creative, list out things you'd like to do for your clients, and do some number crunching on what actually works with direct mail or other approaches you're using in advertising.

Many of the traditional marketing methods, such as press media, don't work as well as they used to. However, we've found that by transitioning a percentage of that budget towards these referral approaches, tremendous benefits can be reaped. Look at it this way, if you don't get any referrals out of your ice cream event, you've still taken a hundred clients out for ice cream, so they still have a positive experience, and something good always comes from that type of upbeat function.

Now let's say you spend that same amount of money on a direct mail campaign or on an advertisement that gets zero response. What would you rather do, interact with a hundred of your clients in a social setting where everyone is happy, or sit in your office waiting for your phone to ring in the wake of a bad ad in a bad publication? The choice seems obvious.

BUSINESS IN A VIRTUAL WORLD

As you can guess, all of this is well and good if all of your clients are in the same geographic area, but how many business owners can say that in this era of teleconferencing and webinars? How, you might be asking, does this approach work in the virtual business world?

Well, ultimately, you are only limited by your own creativity. So the easy answer is, as with anything, don't limit yourself. Think outside the box. How can you reach across the borders? You can start with webinars, Skype, text messaging, email, and phone calls. You name it, and there is probably a communication device that can make it happen. So if you have a client who's on the West Coast and you're on the East Coast, you can still market to that client for referrals, and he can still possibly participate in some events.

Obviously, you're not going to get the same sense of fun and conviviality if people aren't in the same room, but there are ways

You can start with webinars, Skype, text messaging, email, and phone calls.

around that. Perhaps there is a trade show that brings several of your clients to town around the same time once or twice a year. If you have a niche of your clients who do a certain thing and get together once or twice a year, ask them out, or fly to them if it's a big enough client, and pick up the tab for the ten person dinner at Morton's that runs a thousand dollars. If you're traveling to Texas and ten of your clients happen to be in Dallas, schedule a trip to Dallas. You can go anywhere from an evening of ice cream to hiring Tony Bennett.

Or maybe you can set up a video feed of you in California while a client and twenty of his friends are having dinner in New York. It could be a quick call, and you could say something like, "I'm just here to say thanks to my client Bob; and to show that I appreciate all of his confidence and loyalty over the years, I want to pick up the tab for this event, because I couldn't be there in person." There are lots of ways to do things. Again, you are only limited by your own creativity.

MOVING FORWARD

In the beginning of the book I talked about fear of rejection and how a lack of understanding of the power of referrals causes people to walk away from them. However, if you are truly a professional who believes in your product or service, you believe that you have the responsibility to get your message out to as many people as can benefit from that message. The most effective and most inexpensive way to accomplish that is through personal referral.

Because of all the madness that is the 24/7 media onslaught, it's important to make things happen. In a time when Facebook, Twitter, and all other forms of social media have turned communication into a sound bite, if you give me a live person who perhaps could be a potential client of mine and you give me a personal introduction, I have a much better opportunity to do a transaction with them than with someone I've met cold off the street.

This approach works; it's time-tested. I've brought in millions of dollars in fees and commissions over the years by using these approaches, and I continue to use them because they continue to work. I would encourage you to get some of those same results by diving in and trying out some of these methods. Visit our website to get more information on how you can lay out a referral campaign based on your budget, and you could begin seeing results the very next day.

As soon as you can, open your mouth to an

> I've brought in millions of dollars in fees and commissions over the years by using these approaches, and I continue to use them because they continue to work.

So if you visit the website and sign up for the Referral King program, you'll get a ninety day action plan, pieces you can customize to your industry so that you can start getting results.

interesting client and say, "Here's this referral circle that I call the 'You Circle.' Let me show you how it works and, by the way, can you list out five names of people you think could benefit from the service I offer." Examples just like this one are all on the website, providing something that you can put in front of a client immediately, resulting in a referral.

Immediately.

Ultimately, by writing about the power of referrals, I continue to offer quality products and services to the marketplace, to professionals. It makes me sharper as a business person, and I have good karma because I'm showing people how to put more money in their pockets. So if you visit the website and sign up for the Referral King program, you'll get a ninety day action plan, pieces you can customize to your industry so that you can start getting results.

Imagine that. For the cost of one bad advertisement you can get a referral program that has generated millions of dollars, a program that, I believe, will pay for itself twenty to fifty times over if you implement just a few of the ideas.

Once you start utilizing these approaches, you will realize it is your single best return on investment, and you'll put more dollars towards it. Over the years we've put more and more of our marketing budget towards these types of events and programs because they work. There is nothing else that gives you the same bang for your buck. So visit the website, start the Referral King program today, and begin seeing the rewards you and your business deserve.

Once you start utilizing these approaches, you will realize it is your single best return on investment, and you'll put more dollars towards it.

For more information, please visit

www.mikesteranka.com

CPSIA information can be obtained at www.ICGtesting.com
Printed in the USA
BVOW07s0103051213

338243BV00004B/11/P